iPhone 15 Missing

User Manual

Complete Guide for Beginners and Seniors with New Tips and

Tricks

Nick M. Leddy

Copyright

Table Of Contents

Introduction to the iPhone 15

Exploring the iPhone 15: Unveiling Innovation

The world of technology is in a constant state of evolution, with each passing year ushering in new advancements, innovations, and surprises. In this era of rapid technological progress, one name stands tall, capturing the attention and imagination of millions: Apple. Since its inception, Apple has consistently redefined the way we interact with technology, offering a glimpse into the future of smartphones, computers, and devices that seamlessly integrate into our lives. In 2023, Apple takes center stage once again, unveiling its latest masterpiece: the iPhone 15.

As we embark on this journey of discovery, we'll delve deep into the iPhone 15, exploring its groundbreaking features, cutting-edge technology, and the remarkable ways in which it enhances our daily experiences. This comprehensive guide is your window into the world of the iPhone 15, a device that not only represents the pinnacle of engineering but also embodies the relentless pursuit of excellence that has become synonymous with the Apple brand.

A Legacy of Innovation

Before we dive into the iPhone 15, it's essential to acknowledge the rich history and legacy that precedes it. The iPhone, introduced by Apple in 2007, revolutionized the smartphone industry and redefined the concept of a mobile device. From that moment on, iPhones have consistently set the standard for design, performance, and user experience.

Over the years, Apple has introduced numerous iterations and generations of the iPhone, each building upon the successes of its predecessors. With every release, we witnessed the evolution of hardware, the refinement of software, and the introduction of groundbreaking features that left an indelible mark on the tech landscape.

From the introduction of the Retina display to the integration of biometric security features like Touch ID and Face ID, Apple's commitment to innovation has been unwavering. The iPhone has become more than just a communication device; it's a gateway to creativity, productivity, and connectivity. It's a camera, a music player, a gaming console, a health tracker, and a personal assistant—all within the sleek, elegant form factor that we've come to associate with Apple.

The iPhone has also played a pivotal role in shaping how we interact with the digital world. The App Store, which made its debut in 2008, has grown into a vast ecosystem of applications, providing solutions for everything from productivity to entertainment. Whether you're tracking your fitness goals, editing photos, or staying connected with loved ones, there's an app for that.

The Road to iPhone 15

In the lead-up to the iPhone 15's launch, anticipation has been at an all-time high. Apple has a well-deserved reputation for maintaining a shroud of secrecy around its product developments, which only serves to heighten the excitement surrounding each release. Speculation, rumors, and leaks have fueled the imagination of tech enthusiasts, leaving us eager to see what Apple has in store.

While we can't predict every detail about the iPhone 15, we can draw from Apple's history of innovation and its commitment to enhancing the user experience. As we embark on this journey of discovery, it's worth considering the areas in which the iPhone 15 might push the boundaries:

1. Performance: Apple's A-series chips have consistently set the standard for mobile processor performance. With each iteration, we've seen improvements in speed, power efficiency, and AI capabilities. The iPhone 15 is expected to take this to the next level, enabling smoother multitasking, faster app launches, and enhanced gaming experiences.

2. Photography and Videography: The iPhone's camera capabilities have evolved from capturing simple snapshots to professional-grade photography and videography. The iPhone 15 is likely to build on this foundation, offering advancements in low-light photography, AI-driven enhancements, and perhaps even more advanced computational photography features.

3. Display Technology: Apple's commitment to stunning displays with True Tone, ProMotion, and HDR has significantly contributed to the iPhone's visual appeal. The iPhone 15 may introduce further innovations, such as higher refresh rates, improved color accuracy, and advancements in OLED technology.

4. Biometric Security: The iPhone's security features, including Face ID and Touch ID, have been instrumental in safeguarding user data. The iPhone 15 could potentially refine these technologies, making them even more secure and convenient.

5. Connectivity: As the world transitions to 5G networks, the iPhone 15 is expected to embrace this technology fully, offering faster download and upload speeds, lower latency, and improved network performance.

6. Battery Life: Apple has continuously improved the battery life of its iPhones, allowing users to stay connected and productive for longer periods. The iPhone 15 may incorporate advancements in battery technology, optimizing power consumption and reducing the need for frequent charging.

7. Software and Ecosystem: iOS, the operating system that powers iPhones, has evolved with each new release. The iPhone 15 will undoubtedly run the latest iteration of iOS, offering enhancements in user interface, privacy features, and app capabilities. It will seamlessly integrate into the broader Apple ecosystem, allowing users to effortlessly switch between devices and services.

As we explore the iPhone 15 in detail, we'll keep these expectations in mind, understanding that Apple's commitment to innovation extends beyond mere specifications. It encompasses the holistic user experience; from the moment you unbox your device to the countless ways you'll use it in your daily life.

Your Guide to the iPhone 15

This guide is designed to be your companion on your journey with the iPhone 15. Whether you're a longtime iPhone user looking to upgrade or a newcomer to the Apple ecosystem, we'll provide you with a comprehensive understanding of the device's features, functionalities, and capabilities.

We'll begin with the basics, from unboxing and setting up your iPhone 15 to exploring its physical design and user interface. From there, we'll delve into the intricate details of the iPhone 15's features, including its camera system, display technology, and software enhancements. You'll learn how to make the most of your device's capabilities, from taking stunning photos to staying organized and productive.

We'll also cover essential topics like security, privacy, and maintenance, ensuring that your iPhone 15 experience is not only enjoyable but also safe and secure.

Beyond the technical aspects, we'll explore the broader Apple ecosystem, including services like iCloud, the App Store, and connectivity with other Apple devices. You'll discover how the iPhone 15 seamlessly integrates into your digital life, offering a cohesive and efficient user experience.

As we embark on this journey of exploration, innovation, and discovery, we invite you to embrace the possibilities that the iPhone 15 brings to your fingertips. Whether you're using it to capture a breathtaking sunset, connect with loved ones across the globe, or create something entirely new, the iPhone 15 is more than just a device—it's a gateway to limitless possibilities.

So, let's begin our exploration of the iPhone 15, where innovation meets inspiration, and where the future becomes a reality. Welcome to the world of the iPhone 15, where extraordinary experiences await.

Setting Up Your iPhone 15

Setting up your iPhone 15 is the first step towards unlocking its full potential. This section will guide you through the initial setup process, ensuring that you have a seamless experience from the moment you unbox your device.

Unboxing and Physical Overview

Unboxing your iPhone 15 is an exciting moment, but it's essential to

handle the process carefully to avoid any damage to your new device. The packaging of the iPhone is designed with both aesthetics and functionality in mind.

As you open the box, you'll find your iPhone 15 nestled within. Consider the streamlined design and high-end construction for a moment. Beneath the device, you'll discover the accessories, including the charger, earphones, and charging cable. Verify that each component is there and is in good working order.

Once you've inspected the contents, it's time to familiarize yourself with the physical aspects of the iPhone 15. This includes identifying the buttons, ports, and features of the device. For example, you'll find the power button, volume controls, and the lightning port. Understanding the physical layout will help you navigate your iPhone more effectively

Initial Setup and Activation

Now that your iPhone 15 is unboxed and the SIM card is inserted, it's time to power it on and begin the initial setup. The setup process is designed to configure your device according to your preferences and needs.

When you turn on your iPhone 15 for the first time, you'll be greeted by the "Hello" screen. To finish the preliminary setup, follow these steps:

Pick Your Preferred Language and Region: Select your preferred language and region. This will determine the language used throughout the device and set the region-specific settings.

Connect to Wi-Fi or Cellular: To proceed with the setup, you'll need to connect to a Wi-Fi network or use cellular data if your SIM card is active.

Quick Start (if available): If you have an existing iPhone or an iOS device, you can use the Quick Start feature to

set up your new iPhone 15 quickly. Simply bring your old device close to the new one, and follow the on-screen instructions to transfer your data.

Set Up Touch ID or Face ID: Depending on the model of your iPhone 15, you'll have the option to set up biometric authentication.

While Face ID uses facial recognition, Touch ID uses your fingerprint. These features enhance security and convenience when unlocking your device and authorizing purchases.

Create a Passcode: For added security, you can create a passcode or use a longer alphanumeric password to protect your device.

Restore from iCloud or iTunes Backup:

If you're upgrading from a previous iPhone, you can choose to restore your data from an iCloud or iTunes backup. This is a convenient way to transfer your apps, photos, settings, and more to your new device.

16

Set Up Apple ID: To access the full range of Apple services, you'll need an Apple ID. If you already have one, sign in. In the event that

it isn't, you can create a new Apple ID during setup. Your Apple ID is essential for downloading apps from the App Store, using iCloud, and accessing other Apple services.

Enable Location Services: Location services allow apps and services to use your device's location for various purposes, such as navigation and location-based recommendations. This feature can be enabled or disabled for specific apps.

Choose Display Settings: Customize your display settings, including brightness, text size, and display zoom, to suit your preferences.

Set Up Siri: Siri is Apple's virtual assistant. You can choose to enable or disable Siri and set up voice recognition during the initial setup.

Privacy Settings: Take a look at and modify your privacy settings. These settings control how your data is shared with Apple and third-party apps.

Apple Pay (if available): If your iPhone 15 supports Apple Pay, you can set up this convenient payment method during the initial setup.

Screen Time (if available): Screen Time allows you to monitor and manage your screen time and app usage. You can set up Screen Time restrictions during the initial setup.

Once you've completed these steps, your iPhone 15 will be configured and ready to use. The initial setup process ensures that your device is personalized to your liking and provides a seamless user experience.

Restoring from Backup

You can choose to restore your data from a backup if you're upgrading from an earlier iPhone. This can save you time and ensure that your new iPhone 15 has all your important information, apps, and settings.

Follow these procedures to restore data from a backup:

iCloud Backup: If you previously backed up your old iPhone to iCloud, you can select "Restore from iCloud Backup" during the initial setup. Sign in with your Apple ID and choose the most recent backup to restore your data.

iTunes/Finder Backup: If you backed up your old iPhone using iTunes on a computer, connect your new iPhone 15 to the same computer. Open iTunes (or Finder on macOS Catalina and later), and select your new device. Choose "Restore Backup" and select the most recent backup to transfer your data.

Restoring from a backup ensures that your contacts, messages, photos, apps, and other data are seamlessly transferred to your new device, allowing you to pick up where you left off.

Setting Up Touch ID or Face ID

The iPhone 15 offers advanced biometric authentication options: Touch ID and Face ID. These features enhance the security of your device and simplify the process of unlocking it and authorizing purchases.

Setting Up Touch ID:

If your iPhone 15 is equipped with Touch ID, you can set it up during the initial setup or later in the device settings. Here's how to set up Touch ID:

Open the "Settings" app on your iPhone.

After swiping down, choose "Touch ID & Passcode."

Enter your passcode if prompted.

Follow the on-screen instructions to enroll your fingerprint. This typically involves placing your finger on the Touch ID sensor multiple times from different angles.

Once your fingerprint is successfully registered, you can use it to unlock your iPhone, authorize app purchases, and more.

Setting Up Face ID:

If your iPhone 15 features Face ID, you can set it up during the initial setup or later in the device settings. This is how you configure Touch ID:

Launch the iPhone's "Settings" application.

Take a Scroll down and pick "Face ID & Passcode."

Enter your passcode if prompted.

To start the setting procedure, select "Enroll Face".

Position your face within the on-screen frame, and your iPhone will scan your facial features. You'll need to move your head slightly to capture different angles.

Once Face ID is successfully set up, you can use it to unlock your iPhone, authenticate payments, and more.

Both Touch ID and Face ID provide a convenient and secure way to access your iPhone and protect your data. You can choose the method that suits your preferences and device capabilities.

Creating or Logging into an Apple ID

You may access the App Store, iCloud, Apple Music, and other Apple services using your Apple ID as your portal into the Apple ecosystem. If you already have an Apple ID, you can log in during the initial setup. If not, you can create a new one right from your iPhone 15.

Here's how to create or log in to an Apple ID:

Creating a New Apple ID:

If you're new to the Apple ecosystem, follow these steps to create an Apple ID:

During the initial setup, when prompted to sign in with an Apple ID, tap "Don't have an Apple ID or forgot it?"

Select "Create Apple ID."

Enter your first and last name, email address (or create a new one), and a secure password.

Verify your password by entering it again.

Choose your country or region.

Accept the terms and conditions as well as the privacy statement.

Optionally, set up two-factor authentication for added security.

Once your Apple ID is created, you can use it to access various Apple services and personalize your iPhone 15 experience.

Logging into an Existing Apple ID:

If you already have an Apple ID, follow these steps to log in:

During the initial setup, when prompted to sign in with an Apple ID, enter your existing Apple ID email address and password.

To finish the sign-in procedure and confirm your identification, adhere to the on-screen directions.

Logging in with your existing Apple ID ensures that you have access to all your previous app purchases, iCloud storage, and other Apple services. It also makes it easier to set up your device with your existing data.

Navigating the iPhone 15

Once you've successfully set up your iPhone 15, it's time to explore its user interface and navigation features. This section will guide you through the various aspects of navigating your iPhone, ensuring that you can effortlessly access apps, settings, and features.

Home Screen

The Home Screen is the central hub of your iPhone 15, where you'll find all your apps and widgets. Understanding how to navigate and customize the Home Screen is essential for a smooth user experience.

App Icons: The primary elements on the Home Screen are app icons. Each icon represents an app, and tapping on it opens the corresponding app. You can arrange these icons to suit your preferences by moving them or creating app folders.

Widgets: In addition to app icons, you can add widgets to your Home Screen. Widgets provide at-a-glance information and quick access to app features. To add a widget, tap and hold on an empty area of the Home Screen, then tap the "+" icon in the top left corner.

App Library: Swipe to the rightmost screen to access the App Library. This is where all your apps are automatically organized into categories. You can use the search bar at the top to quickly find an app or browse through categories.

Customization: You can customize your Home Screen by rearranging app icons, creating folders, and changing the wallpaper. To move an app icon, tap and hold it until it starts to wiggle, then drag it to a new location. Drag an app icon across another to create a folder. The wallpaper can be changed by going to "Settings" > "Wallpaper."

Control Center

The Control Center is your quick-access panel for essential settings and features. It allows you to adjust various settings without navigating deep into the settings app.

Accessing Control Center: To access the Control Center, swipe down from the top right corner of the screen (or swipe up from the bottom on some models). You can do this from the Home Screen, within apps, or even from the lock screen.

Control Center Features: The Control Center provides shortcuts to settings like Wi-Fi, Bluetooth, Do Not Disturb, screen brightness, volume controls, and more. It also includes toggles for features like Airplane Mode, flashlight, and screen rotation lock.

Customizing Control Center: You can customize the Control Center by adding or removing features. Go to "Settings" > "Control Center" to manage which controls appear here. You can even rearrange their order.

Music Controls: If you're playing music or audio, you'll find playback controls in the Control Center. This allows you to play, pause, skip tracks, and adjust the volume without opening the music app.

Notification Center

The Notification Center is where you'll receive notifications from apps, messages, emails, and more. It also provides widgets for at-a-glance information.

Accessing Notification Center: Swipe down from the top of the screen (or from the top left corner on some models) to access the Notification Center. Here, you'll see a list of your recent notifications.

Notification Types: Notifications can come from various sources, including messages, emails, social media, and apps. You can tap on a notification to open the corresponding app or take action, such as replying to a message.

Widgets: In the Notification Center, you can add widgets that display information from apps or provide quick actions. To add a widget, scroll to the bottom of the Notification Center and tap "Edit."

Clearing Notifications: To clear notifications, swipe right on an individual notification or tap "Clear All" to remove all notifications. You can also manage notification settings for each app in "Settings" > "Notifications."

App Switcher and Multitasking

The App Switcher and multitasking features allow you to switch between apps quickly and efficiently, making it easy to multitask on your iPhone 15.

Accessing the App Switcher: To access the App Switcher, swipe up from the bottom of the screen (or double-click the home button on older models). This displays a list of your recently used apps.

Switching Between Apps: In the App Switcher, you can swipe left or right to scroll through open apps. Tap on an app's card to switch to it. You can also swipe up on an app card to close it.

App Exposé: On some models, you can access App Exposé by tapping and holding an app's card in the App Switcher. This displays all open windows or tabs within that app.

Multitasking Gestures: To quickly switch between recently used apps, swipe left or right along the bottom edge of the screen. You can also switch between apps by swiping up from the bottom and pausing in the middle of the screen to reveal the App Switcher.

Using Gestures and Buttons

Your iPhone 15 relies on a combination of gestures and physical buttons for navigation and control. Understanding these gestures and buttons is crucial for efficient usage.

Home Button (if available): On older iPhone models, you'll have a physical Home button that you can press to return to the Home Screen. You can also use it for tasks like Siri, taking screenshots, and accessing the App Switcher (double-click).

Navigation Gestures: On newer iPhone models without a Home button, navigation is gesture-based. By swiping up from the bottom, you may access the Home Screen. For the App Switcher, swipe up and hold the button. Swipe down from the top left corner for the Control Center, and swipe down from the top right corner for the Notification Center.

Swipe Gestures: Throughout the iPhone interface, you'll use swipe gestures to perform various actions. For example, swipe left or right to switch between app screens, swipe down to dismiss a notification, or swipe left to delete an email.

Pinch and Zoom: In apps like Photos and Safari, you can use pinch gestures to zoom in and out on images or webpages. To zoom in or out, spread two fingers apart or pinch them together.

Siri: Activate Siri by saying "Hey Siri" (if enabled) or pressing and holding the Side button (on models without a Home button) or the Home button (on models with a Home button). You can use Siri for tasks like setting reminders, sending messages, or getting information.

Taking Screenshots: To take a screenshot, press the Side button and the Volume Up button simultaneously. The Photos app will store the screenshot.

Understanding these gestures and button functions will help you navigate your iPhone 15 with ease, making it a powerful tool for communication, productivity, and entertainment.

Managing Apps and Data

Managing apps and data on your iPhone 15 is essential for keeping your device organized, efficient, and clutter-free. In this section, we'll delve into various aspects of app management and data organization.

Installing and Updating Apps

One of the most significant advantages of owning an iPhone is access to a vast library of apps on the App Store. Whether you're looking for productivity tools, entertainment, or utility apps, installing and updating them is a straightforward process.

Installing Apps:

To install apps on your iPhone 15, follow these steps:

Open the "App Store" from your Home Screen.

Search for the app you want to install using the search bar at the bottom.

Tap the app in the search results.

Tap the "Get" button next to the app's name.

If the app requires payment, you'll need to authenticate the purchase with Face ID, Touch ID, or your Apple ID password.

On your device, the app will download and install.

Updating Apps:

Keeping your apps up to date is essential for security and performance improvements. To update apps:

Open the "App Store."

At the top right of the screen, tap your profile photo.

Scroll down to the "Pending Updates" section and tap "Update All" or update individual apps by tapping "Update" next to each app.

You can also enable automatic app updates in "Settings" > "App Store" to ensure that your apps are always up to date without manual intervention.

Organizing Apps

As you accumulate apps on your iPhone 15, it's crucial to keep them organized for easy access. Here are some ways to organize your apps effectively:

Create App Folders:

App folders allow you to group related apps together. To create a folder:

Long-press an app icon on the Home Screen until it starts to wiggle.

Drag one app icon onto another.

A folder will be created, and you can name it according to the category of apps it contains.

Move Apps:

You can rearrange app icons on the Home Screen by long-pressing an app and then dragging it to a new location. This way, you can place your most frequently used apps within easy reach.

App Library:

The App Library, accessible by swiping to the rightmost Home Screen, automatically organizes your apps into categories. You can use the search bar at the top to find apps quickly.

Delete Unwanted Apps:

To declutter your device, you can delete apps you no longer use:

Long-press an app icon until it wiggles.

Tap the "X" in the top-left corner of the app icon.

Confirm the deletion.

Deleting Apps

Deleting apps is a straightforward process, but it's essential to note that when you delete an app, its data may be removed as well. Here's how to delete apps:

Long-press the app icon on the Home Screen until it starts to wiggle.

Tap the "X" on the app icon.

Confirm the deletion.

If you accidentally delete an app and want it back, you can re-download it from the App Store, as long as it's still available.

Managing Contacts

Your iPhone 15 provides a convenient way to manage your contacts, ensuring you can stay connected with friends, family, and colleagues. Here's how to manage your contacts:

Add a Contact:

Follow these Procedures to add a contact manually:

From the Home Screen, Open the "Contacts" app.

Tap the "+" icon in the top right corner.

Enter the contact's details, including name, phone number, email, and more.

Tap "Add" to save the contact.

Import Contacts:

If you're switching from another device, you can import your contacts to your iPhone. You can do this by going to "Settings" > "Contacts" > "Import SIM Contacts" or by using iCloud to sync your contacts.

Edit or Delete Contacts:

To edit or delete a contact:

Open the "Contacts" app.

Tap the contact you want to edit or delete.

To edit, tap "Edit" in the top right corner, make changes, and tap "Done."

To delete, scroll to the bottom of the contact and tap "Delete Contact."

Managing Calendars

The Calendar app on your iPhone 15 allows you to stay organized by managing your events, appointments, and reminders. Here's how to manage your calendars effectively:

Create Events:

To create a new event:

Open the "Calendar" app.

Tap the "+" icon in the top right corner.

Enter event details, including the title, date, time, location, and notes.

Tap "Add" to save the event.

View and Edit Calendars:

You can manage multiple calendars within the Calendar app. To view and edit them:

Open the "Calendar" app.

Tap "Calendars" at the bottom.

Here, you can toggle the visibility of different calendars and color-code them for easy identification.

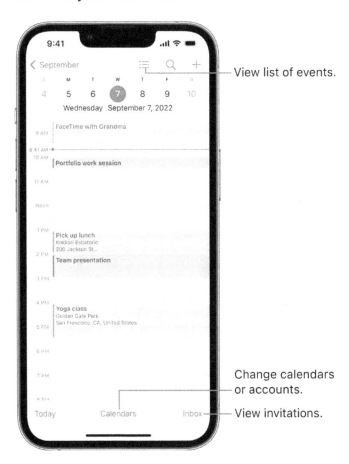

Set Reminders and Alerts:

When creating events or reminders, you can set alerts to receive notifications at specific times. This ensures you don't miss important appointments.

Managing Photos and Videos

Tap to navigate Photos.

Your iPhone 15 is likely to be a repository of precious memories in the form of photos and videos. Managing and organizing them helps you relive those moments effectively:

Photos App:

The Photos app is where all your images and videos are stored. Here's how to manage them:

View Albums: Open the Photos app and tap "Albums" at the bottom to see various albums like Favorites, Recently Deleted, and more.

Create Albums: You can create custom albums to organize your photos. Tap "Albums" > "+" icon to create a new album and add selected photos to it.

Delete Photos and Videos: To delete unwanted photos or videos, open the item, tap the trash icon, and confirm the deletion. Deleted items are moved to the "Recently Deleted" album and can be permanently deleted from there.

Use iCloud Photos: You can enable iCloud Photos to store your photos and videos in the cloud, freeing up space on your device. It may be turned on by going to "Settings" > "[Your Name]" > "iCloud" > "Photos."

Edit Photos: The Photos app also allows you to edit and enhance your photos. Open a photo and tap "Edit" to access editing tools like cropping, filters, and more.

Videos App:

Videos can be found in the Videos app. You can organize and manage your video library by creating playlists, deleting unwanted videos, and using the app's search and sorting features.

Create Playlists: You can create custom playlists to organize your videos by genre, theme, or preference.

Delete Videos: To delete videos, tap and hold on a video in the Videos app, then tap the trash icon and confirm the deletion.

Use Streaming Services: If you prefer not to store videos on your device, consider using streaming services like Apple TV+ and Netflix, which allow you to watch content without downloading it.

By effectively managing your apps and data, including contacts, calendars, photos, and videos, you can ensure that your iPhone 15 remains organized, efficient, and optimized for your needs. Keeping your device clutter-free and well-organized enhances your overall user experience and makes it easier to access the information and content that matters most to you.

Making Calls and Texting

Your iPhone 15 is a powerful communication tool, allowing you to make calls and send text messages seamlessly. In this section, we'll delve into various aspects of making calls and texting on your device.

Making and Receiving Calls

Make the call on another line.

The Phone app on your iPhone 15 serves as the hub for making and receiving calls. Here's how to manage your calls effectively:

Making a Call:

Open the "Phone" app from the Home Screen.

Tap the keypad icon at the bottom to enter a phone number manually.

Enter the phone number you want to call.

Tap the green "Call" button to initiate the call.

Alternatively, you can make calls from your Contacts or Recent Calls list by selecting a contact or number and tapping "Call."

Answering Calls:

When you receive an incoming call, your iPhone 15 will display the caller's name or number if it's in your contacts. To answer the call, simply tap the green "Answer" button. To decline the call, tap the red "Decline" button. You can also respond with a message or set a reminder to call back later.

Using Favorites:

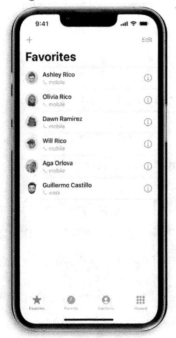

You can add contacts to your Favorites list for quick access. To do this, open a contact and tap "Add to Favorites." Your Favorites list can be accessed from the Phone app, making it convenient to call your most frequent contacts.

Managing Recent Calls:

The "Recent" tab in the Phone app displays your call history. You can view and call back missed calls, review outgoing and incoming calls, and even block unwanted callers.

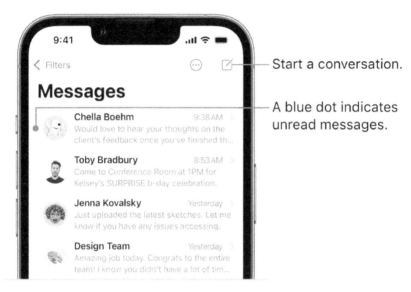

Call Waiting and Holding:

If you're on a call and receive another call, you can use call waiting to switch between calls or merge them into a conference call. To place a call on hold, tap "Hold."

Sending and Receiving Text Messages

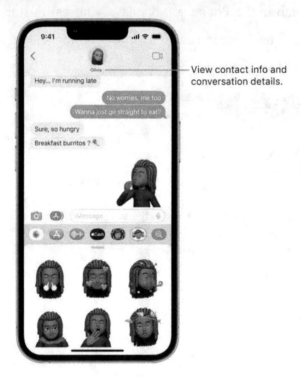

View contact info and conversation details.

Text messaging, or SMS (Short Message Service), is a popular and convenient way to communicate with others. Here's how to send and receive text messages on your iPhone 15:

Sending Text Messages:

Open the "Messages" app from the Home Screen.

Tap the compose icon (usually a pencil or paper and pencil) to start a new message.

Enter the recipient's name or phone number in the "To:" field.

Type your message in the text field at the bottom.

Tap the send icon (usually a blue arrow) to send your message.

iMessage vs. SMS:

Your iPhone 15 uses iMessage to send messages to other Apple devices, which is typically faster and supports additional features like read receipts and multimedia messages. Messages sent to non-Apple devices use SMS.

Receiving Text Messages:

When you receive a text message, you'll see a notification on your lock screen or in the Messages app. Tap the notification to view and respond to the message.

Group Messages:

You can send messages to multiple recipients by creating a group chat. Start a new message, add multiple recipients, and send your message. Group messages can be named, and you can mute or leave group conversations as needed.

Message Attachments:

You can attach photos, videos, documents, and more to your messages. Tap the camera icon to access your camera or the App Store icon to send apps, stickers, and other multimedia content.

Message Settings:

Customize your messaging experience by adjusting settings in the Messages app. You can enable read receipts, change message notification settings, and filter unknown senders.

Using Voicemail

Voicemail is a convenient way to receive and manage missed calls when you're unavailable or unable to answer. Here's how to set up and use voicemail on your iPhone 15:

Setting Up Voicemail:

Open the "Phone" app.

Tap the "Voicemail" tab at the bottom.

Tap "Set Up Now" and create a voicemail password.

Follow the prompts to record your personalized voicemail greeting.

Listening to Voicemail:

When you have a new voicemail, you'll receive a notification. Tap the notification to access your voicemail messages. You can also go to the "Voicemail" tab in the Phone app to listen to your messages.

Managing Voicemail:

You can delete voicemail messages you no longer need or save important ones. Voicemail messages are stored on your device, and you can access them even when offline.

Visual Voicemail:

Visual Voicemail provides a visual interface for managing your voicemail messages. You can see caller information, timestamps, and listen to messages in any order.

Transcription (if available):

Some carriers offer voicemail transcription, which converts voicemail messages into text. This allows you to read your voicemail messages rather than listen to them.

FaceTime and Video Calls

FaceTime is Apple's video and audio calling service, allowing you to connect with friends and family in real-time. Here's how to use FaceTime and make video calls:

Making FaceTime Calls:

Open the "FaceTime" app from the Home Screen.

Tap the "+" icon to start a new call.

Enter the recipient's name or phone number.

Select whether to make a video or audio call.

Tap "Audio" or "Video" to initiate the call.

Receiving FaceTime Calls:

Turn off your mic.

Turn off your camera.

Drag your image to any corner.

Add stickers and other fun effects.

Switch to the rear camera.

Take a Live Photo.

When someone initiates a FaceTime call to you, you'll receive a notification. You can choose to accept or decline the call.

FaceTime Audio:

FaceTime isn't limited to video calls; you can also make high-quality audio calls using FaceTime Audio. This is especially useful when you have a Wi-Fi connection but weak cellular signal.

Group FaceTime Calls:

You can have group FaceTime calls with multiple participants. Start a new FaceTime call, add contacts to the call, and enjoy a group video or audio conversation.

FaceTime Effects and Filters:

FaceTime offers various fun effects and filters that you can use during video calls. You can add stickers, filters, and even use Animoji or Memoji to replace your face with animated characters.

FaceTime Settings:

Customize your FaceTime experience by going to "Settings" > "FaceTime." Here, you can enable or disable FaceTime, adjust call forwarding settings, and set your caller ID.

FaceTime and video call on your iPhone 15 provide a dynamic way to stay connected with friends, family, and colleagues, even when your miles apart. Whether it's a quick audio call, a fun FaceTime conversation, or managing your voicemail, your iPhone 15 is equipped with powerful communication tools to enhance your daily interactions.

Internet and Connectivity

Your iPhone 15 offers a wide range of connectivity options that empower you to stay connected to the internet, and other devices, and maintain your privacy. In this extensive guide, we'll delve into the details of connecting to Wi-Fi networks, utilizing cellular data, managing Bluetooth accessories, sharing files with Air Drop, and enhancing your privacy with VPN and privacy settings.

Connecting to Wi-Fi Networks

Wi-Fi connectivity is essential for fast internet access, especially when you're in the range of a trusted network. Your iPhone 15 makes it easy to connect to Wi-Fi networks securely.

Connecting to Wi-Fi Networks:

In other to connect to a Wi-Fi network, do the following:

From the Home Screen Open the "Settings" app.

Scroll down and tap "Wi-Fi."

Ensure Wi-Fi is turned on.

From the list of accessible networks, choose the preferred Wi-Fi network.

Enter the network password if required.

Tap "Join" or "Connect" to establish the connection.

Once connected, your iPhone 15 will remember the network and automatically connect to it when in range.

Forget a Wi-Fi Network:

To remove a saved Wi-Fi network, go to "Settings" > "Wi-Fi," tap the network name, and select "Forget This Network." This is useful for removing networks you no longer use or trust.

Wi-Fi Assist:

When there is a weak Wi-Fi connection, Wi-Fi Assist automatically switches to cellular data. You can enable or disable this feature in "Settings" > "Cellular" > "Wi-Fi Assist."

Using Cellular Data

Cellular data is crucial for staying connected when Wi-Fi is unavailable. Managing your cellular data usage ensures efficient usage and avoids unexpected charges.

Checking Cellular Data Usage:

To monitor your cellular data usage, navigate to "Settings" > "Cellular." Here, you can view data usage for individual apps and reset data statistics to track usage for a specific period.

Limiting Background Data Usage:

To conserve data, you can restrict background data usage for specific apps. Go to "Settings" > "Cellular" and scroll down to "Cellular Data for Apps." Disable data access for apps that you don't want to use cellular data in the background.

Wi-Fi Assist:

As mentioned earlier, Wi-Fi Assist helps maintain a stable internet connection by switching to cellular data when Wi-Fi is weak. However, be mindful of your data plan when using this feature.

Data Roaming:

When traveling internationally, be cautious about data roaming charges. You can enable or disable data roaming in "Settings" > "Cellular" > "Cellular Data Options."

Bluetooth and Accessories

Bluetooth connectivity allows you to connect your iPhone 15 to a variety of accessories and devices, including headphones, speakers, smartwatches, and more.

Pairing Bluetooth Accessories:

To pair a Bluetooth accessory, follow these steps:

Open the "Settings" app.

Tap "Bluetooth."

Ensure Bluetooth is turned on.

Put your accessory into pairing mode (refer to the accessory's manual).

Wait for your accessory to appear in the list of available devices.

Tap the accessory name to pair it with your iPhone.

Once paired, your iPhone 15 will remember the accessory for future connections.

Managing Bluetooth Devices:

To manage paired Bluetooth devices, go to "Settings" > "Bluetooth." Here, you can connect or disconnect devices and forget previously paired accessories.

Bluetooth Settings:

Under "Settings" > "Bluetooth," you can customize settings for each paired device. This includes adjusting audio routing, enabling notifications, and more.

AirDrop and File Sharing

AirDrop is a powerful feature that allows you to share files, photos, videos, and more with nearby Apple devices seamlessly.

Using AirDrop:

To use AirDrop, follow these steps:

Ensure Wi-Fi and Bluetooth are turned on for both devices.

Open the file or item you want to share.

Tap the Share icon (usually represented by an arrow).

In the sharing options, select the recipient's device under "AirDrop."

A notification inviting the recipient to accept or reject the file will be sent. Once accepted, the file is transferred directly between devices.

AirDrop Privacy Settings:

You can configure your AirDrop settings for "Contacts Only" or "Everyone." "Contacts Only" limits AirDrop access to people in your contacts, while "Everyone" allows anyone nearby to send you files. Adjust these settings in "Settings" > "General" > "AirDrop."

Receiving AirDrop Files:

You'll get a notification if someone sends you a file using AirDrop. Tap "Accept" to receive the file, and it will be saved in the respective app or location.

VPN and Privacy Settings

Maintaining your privacy and security while using the internet is paramount. Your iPhone 15 offers several privacy features, including VPN support and various settings for enhancing your privacy.

VPN (Virtual Private Network):

VPNs enhance your online privacy and security by encrypting your internet connection. To set up a VPN on your iPhone 15, follow these steps:

Open "Settings."

Scroll down and tap "VPN."

Tap "Add VPN Configuration" and enter the VPN details provided by your VPN service provider.

Tap "Done" to save the configuration.

You can connect to or disconnect from your VPN in the "VPN" section of the "Settings" app.

Privacy Settings:

To manage privacy settings on your iPhone 15, navigate to "Settings" > "Privacy." Here, you'll find various categories, including Location Services, Contacts, Photos, and more, allowing you to control app access to your personal data.

App Tracking Transparency:

With iOS 14 and later, App Tracking Transparency gives you the option to allow or deny apps from tracking your activity across other apps and websites. When an app wants to track you, you'll receive a pop-up notification asking for your permission.

Safari Privacy Settings:

In the Safari browser, you can enhance your privacy by enabling features such as "Prevent Cross-Site Tracking" and "Block All Cookies." These settings can be configured in "Settings" > "Safari."

Privacy Reports:

Safari also provides Privacy Reports, allowing you to see which websites have trackers and how often they are blocked. Access this feature by tapping the "AA" icon in the address bar and selecting "Privacy Report."

Location Services:

In "Settings" > "Privacy" > "Location Services," you can control which apps have access to your location and customize location sharing preferences.

By understanding and utilizing these internet and connectivity features on your iPhone 15, you can optimize your device for fast, secure, and private online experiences. Whether it's connecting to Wi-Fi networks, managing cellular data, pairing Bluetooth accessories, sharing files with AirDrop, or enhancing your privacy with VPN and privacy settings, your iPhone 15 empowers you to stay connected and protected in the digital world.

Email and Messaging

Email and messaging are fundamental aspects of communication on your iPhone 15. In this extensive guide, we'll delve into the details of setting up email accounts, using the Mail app effectively, managing messages and conversations, and maximizing the power of iMessage and group chats.

Setting Up Email Accounts

Your iPhone 15 allows you to configure and manage various email accounts, whether they are personal, work-related, or from different email service providers. Setting up these accounts ensures that you can access and manage your emails efficiently.

Adding an Email Account:

To add an email account, follow these steps:

Open the "Settings" app from your Home Screen.

Scroll down and tap "Mail."

Tap "Accounts."

Tap "Add Account."

Select your email provider (e.g., iCloud, Google, Microsoft Exchange, Yahoo).

Follow the on-screen instructions to enter your email address, password, and other required information.

Tap "Next" or "Sign In" to verify the account.

Your iPhone 15 will configure the settings automatically for many popular email providers, but you may need to enter manual server details for some accounts.

Multiple Email Accounts:

You can add multiple email accounts to your iPhone 15. This is useful for managing personal, work, and other email addresses all in one place. Repeat the above steps to add additional accounts.

Custom Email Settings:

For accounts that require manual configuration, such as Microsoft Exchange or custom domains, you can enter the server details by selecting "Other" in the email provider list.

Using the Mail App

The Mail app on your iPhone 15 is a powerful tool for managing your email accounts and messages efficiently. Here are some pointers to get the most of it:

Navigating the Mail App:

When you open the Mail app, you'll see your Inbox, where all your received emails are listed. You can access other folders like Sent, Drafts, Trash, and more by tapping "Mailboxes" in the top-left corner.

Composing Emails:

To compose a new email, tap the compose icon (usually represented by a pencil or paper and pencil). Type in the subject line, sender email address, and body of your message. You can also attach files, photos, and documents to your emails.

Reading and Responding to Emails:

Tap an email in your Inbox to open and read it. To reply, forward, or delete an email, tap the respective icons at the bottom of the email.

Additionally, emails can be marked as read or unread.

Change mailboxes or accounts.

Delete, move, or mark multiple messages.

Compose a message.

Filter messages.

Organizing Emails:

You can organize your emails by creating folders or labels. To do this, tap "Edit" in the Mailboxes section and select "New Mailbox" or "New Mailbox Folder." You can move emails into these folders for better organization.

Search Function:

To locate certain emails or contacts quickly, use the search bar at the top. Your iPhone 15 will search through your emails and display relevant results.

Swipe Actions:

Customize swipe actions in the Mail app settings. For example, you can set swiping left to mark emails as read or unread and swiping right to delete or archive them.

Using Multiple Email Accounts:

You can easily switch between multiple email accounts within the Mail app. Tap your email address in the upper-left corner to access the account list.

Notifications and Alerts:

Customize email notifications and alerts in the "Settings" app under "Mail." You can choose how and when you want to receive email notifications.

Managing Messages and Conversations

Managing messages and email conversations efficiently is crucial for staying organized and responsive. Here are some tips for managing your messages effectively:

Conversation View:

The Mail app groups related emails into conversations, making it easier to track the flow of a discussion. You can enable or disable this feature in the Mail app settings.

Flagging Emails:

Flagging important emails helps you keep track of them. To flag an email, open it and tap the flag icon. You can then access flagged emails in the "Flagged" mailbox.

Archiving and Deleting:

To clear the clutter from your Inbox, you can archive or delete emails. Archiving removes them from the Inbox but keeps them in the All-Mail folder. Deleting permanently removes them. Swipe left on an email to access these options.

Managing Attachments:

You can save email attachments to your iPhone by tapping and holding the attachment in the email. You can then choose to save it to your iCloud Drive or another location.

Custom Mailbox Folders:

Create custom mailbox folders to organize emails according to your preferences. If you have several email accounts, this is really helpful.

Using iMessage and Group Chats

iMessage is Apple's proprietary messaging platform, offering a rich and interactive messaging experience. Group chats allow you to communicate with multiple contacts simultaneously.

Setting Up iMessage:

iMessage is usually set up automatically when you activate your iPhone 15 with an Apple ID. To confirm or set up iMessage:

Open the "Settings" app.

Scroll down and tap "Messages."

Ensure iMessage is turned on.

Sending iMessages:

To send an iMessage, open the "Messages" app, tap the compose icon, and start typing the recipient's name or phone number. iMessage is indicated by a blue send button, while regular text messages (SMS) use a green send button.

Group Chats:

Group chats in iMessage allow you to communicate with multiple contacts at once. To start a group chat:

Open the "Messages" app.

Tap the compose icon.

Enter the names or phone numbers of the recipients.

Compose your message, and it will be sent to all recipients in the group.

Memoji and Animoji:

iMessage offers fun features like Memoji and Animoji, which allow you to send animated characters that mimic your facial expressions and voice. Access these features by tapping the "A" icon next to the text field.

Message Effects:

iMessage includes message effects like balloons, confetti, and fireworks. To use them, type your message, then press and hold the send button to access the effects menu.

Message Reactions:

You can react to messages with thumbs up, thumbs down, or other emojis by long-pressing a message and selecting a reaction.

Tapback:

Tapback allows you to quickly respond to a message with a thumbs up, thumbs down, a heart, and other icons. Double-tap a message to access these options.

Managing Group Chats:

You can customize group chats by giving them a name, muting notifications, and even leaving the group if you no longer wish to participate.

Mastering the art of email and messaging on your iPhone 15 is essential for staying connected and organized. Whether you're setting up email accounts, using the Mail app, managing messages and conversations, or harnessing the power of iMessage and group chats, your iPhone 15 provides you with the tools to communicate effectively and efficiently.

Personalization and Settings

Your iPhone 15 offers a wide range of personalization options and settings that allow you to tailor your device to your preferences, enhance accessibility, manage battery and power efficiently, enhance security and privacy, and utilize iCloud for backups and data storage. In this extensive guide, we'll delve into each of these aspects.

Customizing Your iPhone

Personalizing your iPhone 15 is about making the device uniquely yours, from the Home Screen to sounds and wallpapers.

Home Screen Customization:

App Icons: You can organize your apps by creating folders, moving icons, or hiding them from the Home Screen. To access editing mode, tap and hold an app icon.

Widgets: iOS 14 and later allow you to add widgets to your Home Screen for quick access to information. Tap and hold the Home Screen, then tap the "+" icon in the top-left corner to add widgets.

App Library: The App Library organizes your apps automatically, making it easier to find and access them. Swipe left from the last Home Screen page to access the App Library.

Wallpapers:

- **Dynamic and Live Wallpapers:** iOS offers dynamic and live wallpapers that move and respond to touch. You can select these in "Settings" > "Wallpaper."
- **Custom Wallpapers:** You can use your photos as wallpapers by choosing a picture in the Photos app, tapping the share icon, and selecting "Use as Wallpaper."

Sounds and Ringtones:

- **Custom Ringtones:** You can assign custom ringtones to contacts by editing a contact's details and selecting a ringtone.
- **Notification Sounds:** Customize notification sounds for individual apps in "Settings" > "Sounds & Haptics."

Dark Mode:

iOS offers a Dark Mode that changes the system and app interfaces to darker colors, which can be easier on the eyes, save battery life, and enhance visibility in low-light environments. Enable it in "Settings" > "Display & Brightness."

Accessibility Features

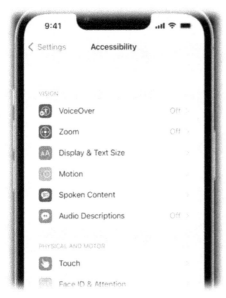

iOS is known for its comprehensive accessibility features designed to make the device usable by individuals with various needs. These features enhance usability for everyone. Here are some key accessibility features:

VoiceOver:

VoiceOver is a screen reader that reads aloud what's on the screen, making it accessible to visually impaired users. Enable it in "Settings" > "Accessibility" > "VoiceOver."

Magnifier:

The Magnifier feature uses the iPhone's camera to magnify text and objects. Activate it in "Settings" > "Accessibility" > "Magnifier."

Zoom:

Zoom allows you to magnify the entire screen or a portion of it by double-tapping the screen with three fingers. Enable it in "Settings" > "Accessibility" > "Zoom."

Display Accommodations:

These settings include options for color filters, invert colors, and reduce white point to customize the display for different visual preferences.

Speech:

iOS provides a Speak Screen option, which reads the content of the screen aloud when you swipe down with two fingers from the top of the screen.

Subtitles and Captioning:

You can enable closed captions and subtitles in various apps and customize their appearance.

AssistiveTouch:

AssistiveTouch provides an on-screen menu with touch gestures, making it easier to interact with the device for individuals with motor skill challenges.

Sound Recognition:

Sound Recognition detects specific sounds like alarms, sirens, or doorbells and sends a notification to the user.

Touch Accommodations:

Customize touch sensitivity and duration for taps and presses to accommodate different touch preferences.

Battery and Power Management

Effectively managing your iPhone's battery life ensures that your device lasts throughout the day. Here are some tips and settings to optimize battery performance:

Battery Usage Information:

View which apps are consuming the most battery by going to "Settings" > "Battery." This helps you identify apps that may need optimization.

Low Power Mode:

Activate Low Power Mode in "Settings" > "Battery" to reduce background activity and extend battery life when your device's charge is running low.

Background App Refresh:

Disable background app refresh for apps that don't require constant updates. Configure this in "Settings" > "General" > "Background App Refresh."

Auto-Lock:

Shorten the auto-lock period to turn off the screen sooner when your device is not in use. Open "Settings" and select "Display & Brightness" then "Auto-Lock."

Display Settings:

Adjust the screen brightness and enable "True Tone" to match the ambient lighting conditions, conserving power.

App Push Notifications:

Reduce the number of app push notifications to minimize screen wake-ups and save battery life. Manage notifications in "Settings" > "Notifications."

Battery Health:

Check the health of your iPhone's battery in "Settings" > "Battery" > "Battery Health." If the maximum capacity is significantly reduced, consider replacing the battery.

Background Location Tracking:

Review app location tracking settings in "Settings" > "Privacy" > "Location Services" to ensure apps are not continuously tracking your location in the background.

Security and Privacy Settings

Privacy and personal data security are of highest significance. iPhone 15 provides robust security and privacy settings to keep your information safe:

Face ID and Touch ID:

Enable Face ID or Touch ID for secure and convenient device unlocking and app access. Set up these features in "Settings" > "Face ID & Passcode" or "Touch ID & Passcode."

Passcode and Security:

Create a strong passcode for added security. You can configure passcode settings in "Settings" > "Face ID & Passcode" or "Touch ID & Passcode."

App Permissions:

Review and manage app permissions for location, camera, microphone, and other sensitive data in "Settings" > "Privacy."

Two-Factor Authentication:

Enhance your Apple ID's security with two-factor authentication (2FA) to prevent unauthorized access. Set up 2FA in "Settings" > [Your Name] > "Password & Security" > "Two-Factor Authentication."

App Tracking Transparency:

iOS 14 and later include App Tracking Transparency, which allows you to control whether apps can track your activity across other apps and websites. Configure this in "Settings" > "Privacy" > "Tracking."

Find My iPhone:

Enable Find My iPhone to locate your device if it's lost or stolen. You can also remotely lock or erase your device using this feature.

Safari Privacy Settings:

In Safari, you can block cross-site tracking and prevent websites from requesting tracking permissions. Customize these settings in "Settings" > "Safari."

iCloud and Backup Options

iCloud is Apple's cloud storage and synchronization service that keeps your data, photos, and documents up to date across all your devices. Here's how to make the most of iCloud and ensure your data is backed up:

iCloud Backup:

Enable iCloud Backup to automatically back up your device, including apps, settings, and photos. Configure this in "Settings" > [Your Name] > "iCloud" > "iCloud Backup."

Photos and Videos:

Use iCloud Photos to store and access your photos and videos across all your devices Go to "Settings" > "iCloud Photos" and turn it on. "iCloud" > "Photos" > [Your Name].

App Data and Settings:

Some apps offer iCloud synchronization to keep your data and settings consistent across devices. Check app-specific settings for this feature.

iCloud Drive:

iCloud Drive allows you to store documents and files in the cloud and access them from any device. Enable iCloud Drive in "Settings" > [Your Name] > "iCloud" > "iCloud Drive."

Keychain:

iCloud Keychain securely stores your passwords and payment information, syncing them across your Apple devices. Activate it in "Settings" > [Your Name] > "iCloud" > "Keychain."

Find My iPhone:

Enable Find My iPhone in "Settings" > [Your Name] > "Find My" to help locate your device if it's lost or stolen.

iCloud Storage:

Manage your iCloud storage in "Settings" > [Your Name] > "iCloud" > "Manage Storage." You can upgrade your storage plan if needed.

By understanding and utilizing the personalization and settings options on your iPhone 15, you can make your device truly your own, enhance accessibility, optimize battery life, protect your security and privacy, and seamlessly back up your data with iCloud. These features empower you to make the most of your iPhone while ensuring a personalized and secure user experience.

Entertainment and Multimedia

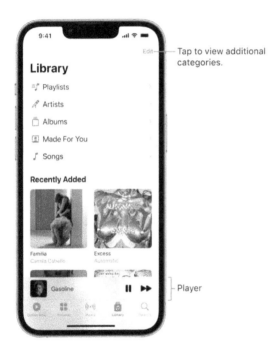

Tap to view additional categories.

Player

Your iPhone 15 is a versatile device that offers a wide range of entertainment and multimedia options. In this extensive guide, we'll delve into the details of playing music and podcasts, watching videos and streaming content, using the camera and managing photos, and exploring the world of augmented reality (AR) apps.

Playing Music and Podcasts

Your iPhone 15 serves as a portable music and podcast player, allowing you to enjoy your favorite tunes and stay up-to-date with the latest podcasts.

Apple Music:

Apple Music offers a vast library of songs and playlists. You can subscribe to Apple Music and access a vast catalog, or simply use the Music app to play songs purchased or synced from your computer.

Music Playback:

Open the Music app and navigate through your library, playlists, and artists to find the music you want to listen to. Tap a song to start playback.

Creating Playlists:

To arrange your music, you can make personalized playlists. Tap "New Playlist" in the Library section of the Music app, add songs, and name your playlist.

Podcasts:

The Podcasts app allows you to explore, subscribe to, and listen to podcasts on various topics. You can search for specific podcasts or browse categories.

Apple Music and Podcast Settings:

Customize your music and podcast settings in the Settings app. You can configure audio quality, download options, and more.

Siri Integration:

Use Siri to control your music and podcasts by saying commands like "Play my favorite playlist" or "Skip to the next track."

Watching Videos and Streaming

Your iPhone 15 is a mini entertainment center, perfect for watching videos and streaming content on the go.

Video Playback:

The Videos app allows you to watch movies and TV shows that you've purchased or rented from the iTunes Store. Simply open the app, select your video, and enjoy.

Streaming Services:

There are various streaming services available for your iPhone 15, including Netflix, Hulu, Disney+, Amazon Prime Video, and more. Download the respective apps from the App Store and subscribe to the service of your choice.

YouTube:

The YouTube app is a popular choice for watching a wide variety of content. You can browse, search, and subscribe to channels on YouTube.

Video Settings:

Customize video settings like screen brightness, volume, and closed captioning in the Control Center while watching a video.

Screen Mirroring:

You can mirror your iPhone's screen to a compatible TV or streaming device using AirPlay. This is useful for watching content on a larger screen.

Using the Camera and Photos

Your iPhone 15 features a powerful camera that lets you capture stunning photos and videos Make the most of it by following these tips:

Camera Modes:

The Camera app offers various modes like Photo, Portrait, Video, and more. Swipe left or right to switch between modes.

Taking Photos:

To take a photo, open the Camera app, frame your shot, and tap the shutter button. You can also use the volume buttons or a connected headset to take pictures.

Portrait Mode:

Portrait Mode creates professional-looking photos with a blurred background, simulating the effect of a DSLR camera. It's ideal for capturing stunning portraits.

Night Mode:

Night Mode enhances low-light photography. When your iPhone detects low light, it will automatically enable Night Mode Additionally, you can manually change the intensity.

Live Photos:

Live Photos include a brief film clip that is recorded with the picture. To enable or disable Live Photos, tap the icon at the top of the Camera app.

Editing Photos:

You can edit and enhance your photos directly in the Photos app. Open a photo, tap "Edit," and use the editing tools to adjust brightness, color, and more.

Using iCloud Photos:

iCloud Photos syncs your photos and videos across all your Apple devices. Enable it in "Settings" > [Your Name] > "iCloud" > "Photos."

Managing Albums:

Arrange your pictures into albums for convenient viewing. Create albums based on events, people, or themes.

AR and Augmented Reality Apps

Augmented Reality (AR) apps offer immersive and interactive experiences on your iPhone 15. Here's how to explore the world of **AR:**

Downloading AR Apps:

Visit the App Store and search for AR apps in various categories, including gaming, education, and utility.

Measure App:

The Measure app uses AR to measure objects and distances. Open the Measure app and follow the on-screen instructions to take measurements.

AR Gaming:

Many games incorporate AR features for a unique gaming experience. Look for games that support ARKit, Apple's AR development framework.

Educational AR:

AR can be a powerful educational tool. Explore AR apps that help you learn about astronomy, anatomy, history, and more.

Shopping and AR:

Some retail apps offer AR shopping experiences, allowing you to visualize products in your environment before making a purchase.

Exploring ARKit:

ARKit is Apple's platform for AR app development. It enables developers to create innovative AR experiences. Check out the latest AR apps and games on the App Store to see the potential of ARKit.

The entertainment and multimedia capabilities of your iPhone 15 are vast and diverse. Whether you're enjoying music and podcasts, watching videos and streaming content, capturing photos and videos with the camera, or immersing yourself in augmented reality apps, your iPhone 15 provides a wealth of entertainment options at your fingertips. Explore these features to make the most of your device's multimedia capabilities.

Productivity and Apps

Your iPhone 15 is a powerful tool for boosting productivity, with a vast array of apps designed to help you work efficiently, stay organized, and take care of your health and fitness. In this extensive guide, we'll delve into the details of using productivity apps, note-taking and document editing, time management and reminders, and health and fitness apps.

Using Productivity Apps

Productivity apps are designed to streamline your work and help you get things done more efficiently. Here's how to make the most of them:

Apple's Productivity Suite:

Your iPhone 15 comes with a suite of built-in productivity apps like Notes, Reminders, Calendar, and Files. Familiarize yourself with these apps as they are tightly integrated into the iOS ecosystem.

Third-Party Productivity Apps:

Explore the App Store for third-party productivity apps that cater to your specific needs. Whether it's task management, note-taking, or project planning, there are apps available for almost every purpose.

Task Management:

Task management apps like To do list, Microsoft To Do, and Things allow you to create, organize, and prioritize tasks and to-do lists.

Project Management:

Apps like Trello, Asana, and Basecamp are excellent for managing larger projects with multiple tasks, deadlines, and collaborators.

Cloud Storage and File Management:

Utilize cloud storage services like iCloud Drive, Dropbox, Google Drive, and Microsoft OneDrive to access your files from anywhere.

Collaborative Work:

Apps such as Slack and Microsoft Teams facilitate team communication, file sharing, and collaboration in real-time.

Email Management:

Consider using email management apps like Outlook, Spark, or Edison Mail to declutter your inbox and boost email productivity.

Note-Taking and Document Editing

Your iPhone 15 makes it easy to take notes, edit documents, and stay organized:

Notes App:

The built-in Notes app offers a powerful and easy-to-use platform for taking notes. You can create different note categories, format text, add images and sketches, and even scan documents.

Third-Party Note-Taking Apps:

Apps like Evernote, Notion, and OneNote provide advanced note-taking features and organization tools.

Document Editing:

Use apps like Microsoft Word, Google Docs, and Pages for document editing and collaboration. These apps allow you to create, edit, and format documents on the go.

Scanning Documents:

The Notes app includes a document scanning feature. Open a note, tap the camera icon, and select "Scan Documents" to capture and save documents.

PDF Annotation:

Apps like Adobe Acrobat Reader and PDF Expert enable you to annotate and sign PDFs directly on your iPhone.

Time Management and Reminders

Managing your time effectively and setting reminders is essential for staying organized and meeting deadlines:

Calendar App:

View list of events.

Change calendars or accounts.

View invitations.

The Calendar app helps you schedule events, appointments, and meetings. You can also create multiple calendars for different aspects of your life

Siri Integration:

Use Siri to create calendar events and set reminders with voice commands. For instance, you may tell Siri to "Hey Siri, schedule a meeting for tomorrow at 2 PM."

Reminders App:

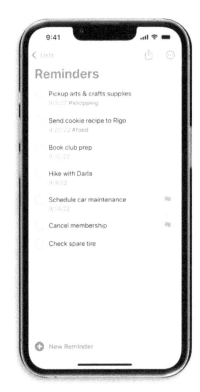

The Reminders app allows you to create to-do lists and set reminders with due dates. You can organize tasks into different lists and prioritize them.

Location-Based Reminders:

Set reminders that trigger when you arrive at or leave a specific location. For instance, you can create a reminder to pick up groceries when you leave work.

Third-Party Task Managers:

Explore third-party task management apps like Wunderlist, Anydo, and to do list for advanced features and integration with other productivity apps.

Time Tracking:

Use time tracking apps like Toggl or Clockify to monitor how you spend your time on tasks and projects.

Health and Fitness Apps

Your iPhone 15 can help you lead a healthier lifestyle with the help of health and fitness apps:

Health App:

The health app is your central hub for tracking health and fitness data. It can monitor your steps, heart rate, sleep, and more. It also integrates with third-party health apps and devices.

Fitness Tracking:

Use the built-in Activity app to set fitness goals, track workouts, and monitor your progress. It's a great tool for staying active and motivated.

Nutrition Tracking:

Apps like MyFitnessPal and Lose It! allow you to track your food intake, count calories, and monitor your nutritional goals.

Meditation and Mindfulness:

Apps like Calm and Headspace offer guided meditation and mindfulness exercises to reduce stress and improve mental well-being.

Sleep Tracking:

Monitor your sleep patterns and quality using apps like Sleep Cycle or Auto Sleep. These apps provide insights into your sleep habits.

Water Intake:

Stay hydrated by tracking your water intake with apps like Water Minder. They remind you to drink water at regular intervals.

Workout Apps:

Explore workout apps like Nike Training Club, Fit bod, and Yoga for Beginners to find exercise routines that suit your fitness goals.

Wearable Fitness Devices:

Consider pairing your iPhone 15 with a fitness wearable like the Apple Watch to track your health and fitness data more accurately.

By harnessing the power of productivity apps, note-taking and document editing tools, effective time management, and health and fitness apps, your iPhone 15 can become an invaluable asset for both work and personal life. Whether you're boosting productivity, staying organized, or improving your health, your iPhone 15 is your go-to device for enhanced productivity and well-being.

Troubleshooting and Support

Your iPhone 15 is a powerful and sophisticated device, but like any technology, it may encounter issues from time to time. In this extensive guide, we'll cover common issues and solutions, how to get help from Apple Support and important information about your device's warranty and service options.

Common Issues and Solutions

Even the most advanced devices can experience common problems. Here are some common issues that iPhone users may encounter and the solutions to resolve them:

Battery Drains Quickly:

Solution: Check which apps are consuming the most battery by going to "Settings" > "Battery." You can limit background app refresh and reduce screen brightness to save power. If the battery issue persists, consider having the battery checked by Apple.

Slow Performance:

Solution: Close background apps by double-clicking the Home button (or swiping up from the bottom on models without a Home button) and swiping away apps. Clear storage space by deleting unnecessary apps or files. If performance issues continue, try restarting your device.

Connectivity Problems:

Solution: If you have Wi-Fi issues, restart your router or modem. For cellular issues, toggle Airplane Mode on and off. If the issue persists, check for software updates and reset network settings in "Settings" > "General" > "Reset."

App Crashes:

Solution: Update the problematic app to the latest version from the App Store. If it still crashes, try deleting and reinstalling the app. Sometimes, an iOS update can resolve compatibility issues.

Frozen or Unresponsive Screen:

Solution: Force restart your iPhone by quickly pressing and releasing the Volume Up button, followed by the Volume Down button, and then holding the Side (or Power) button until you see the Apple logo.

Touchscreen Issues:

Solution: Clean the screen to remove dirt or smudges. If touch responsiveness is still a problem, restart your iPhone or update to the latest iOS version.

Lost or Deleted Data:

Solution: If you have a backup on iCloud or iTunes, you can restore lost data. To prevent data loss, regularly back up your iPhone. Backups can be made using iTunes or iCloud Backup.

Bluetooth Connectivity Problems:

Solution: Make sure Bluetooth is turned on in "Settings" > "Bluetooth." Forget and re-pair the device you're trying to connect to. If issues persist, restart your iPhone.

No Sound or Low Volume:

Solution: Check the volume settings and ensure the Do Not Disturb mode is off. Clean the speaker grills and headphone jack. If sound issues continue, check the device's sound settings in "Settings" > "Sound & Haptics."

Overheating:

Solution: Avoid exposing your iPhone to extreme temperatures. Close background apps and keep your device in a well-ventilated area. If overheating is a recurring issue, contact Apple Support.

Getting Help from Apple Support

If you encounter an issue that you can't resolve on your own, Apple offers various support options to assist you:

Apple Support Website:

Visit the Apple Support website (support.apple.com) for articles, guides, and troubleshooting tips for common issues. Simply enter your question or problem in the search bar to find relevant information.

Apple Support App:

Download the Apple Support app from the App Store to access personalized support, schedule appointments, and chat with Apple experts. The app also allows you to see your device's warranty status.

Contacting Apple Support:

If you need direct assistance, you can contact Apple Support by phone, chat, or email. Visit the Apple Support website and click on "Contact Apple Support" to find contact options and availability in your region.

Genius Bar Appointments:

If you have an Apple Store nearby, you can schedule an appointment at the Genius Bar for in-person support. Apple's skilled technicians can diagnose and resolve hardware and software issues.

Community and Forums:

Apple has an active user community and support forums where you can ask questions and get advice from other Apple users and experts.

Warranty and Service Information

Understanding your iPhone's warranty and service options is essential for addressing hardware issues and device repairs.

Limited Warranty:

Your iPhone comes with a limited warranty that covers manufacturing defects and hardware issues for one year from the date of purchase. This warranty is automatically included with your device and provides free repairs for eligible issues.

AppleCare+:

Apple offers an extended warranty and service plan called AppleCare+. With AppleCare+, you can extend your coverage for up to two years from the original purchase date. It also includes coverage for accidental damage, subject to a deductible.

AppleCare Protection Plan:

If AppleCare+ isn't available in your region, you may have access to the AppleCare Protection Plan, which offers extended warranty coverage without accidental damage protection.

Out-of-Warranty Service:

If your iPhone is no longer covered by warranty, you can still receive service from Apple. Apple provides repair and replacement services for a fee, depending on the issue and your device's condition.

Battery Service:

If your iPhone's battery experiences significant degradation and it's still under warranty or covered by AppleCare+, Apple may offer a battery replacement service at no additional cost.

Authorized Service Providers:

Apple has a network of authorized service providers where you can receive repair and service assistance. These companies use authentic Apple parts and have undergone training from Apple.

Check Warranty Status:

To check your iPhone's warranty status, visit the Apple Support website or use the Apple Support app. You'll need your device's serial number, which can be found in "Settings" > "General" > "About."

Apple's Repair Process:

If you need a repair or replacement, Apple provides a straightforward and efficient process. You can start a repair request online, schedule an appointment, or visit an Apple Store or authorized service provider.

Understanding your iPhone's warranty coverage and service options ensures that you can address hardware issues promptly and effectively. Whether your device is under warranty or not, Apple provides various support channels to help you resolve problems and keep your iPhone functioning at its best.

Advanced Tips and Tricks

Your iPhone 15 is packed with advanced features and hidden shortcuts that can enhance your user experience and productivity. In this comprehensive guide, we'll explore advanced features, shortcuts, iOS updates, and new features to help you unlock the full potential of your device.

Advanced Features and Shortcuts

Your iPhone 15 offers a range of advanced features and shortcuts that can significantly improve your daily interactions with the device. Let's explore some of these advanced capabilities:

Face ID and Touch ID Tips:

Unlock with a Glance: Face ID can recognize your face even when you're wearing glasses or a hat. It adapts to changes in your appearance over time.

Alternative Appearance: Set up an alternative appearance in Face ID settings to recognize different looks or even a trusted person's face.

Faster Unlock: Swipe up from the bottom of the screen after Face ID recognizes your face to skip the swipe gesture.

Quick Actions and 3D Touch (if available):

App Quick Actions: Press firmly on app icons to reveal quick actions, such as "Take a Selfie" for the Camera app or "New Message" for Messages.

Peek and Pop: Use 3D Touch to peek into emails, links, or messages without fully opening them. To pop into the material, press more firmly.

Keyboard Shortcuts:

Keyboard Trackpad: On devices with 3D Touch or Haptic Touch, press and hold the keyboard to turn it into a trackpad for precise cursor control.

Quick Text Selection: Double-tap the Shift key to enable Caps Lock. Triple-tap to select an entire sentence. Quadruple-tap for a whole paragraph.

Customizing Control Center:

Add Controls: Customize the Control Center by adding or removing controls like Screen Recording, Magnifier, or Hearing.

Access in Apps: Swipe down from the top-right corner of the screen to access Control Center, even while in apps.

Advanced Siri Commands:

Shortcuts: Create Siri shortcuts in the Shortcuts app to automate tasks. For example, "Hey Siri, I'm heading home" can trigger your navigation app and send a message to let someone know you're on your way.

Camera Features:

ProRAW and ProRes Video: On supported models, you can capture photos in ProRAW and ProRes video for more advanced editing options.

Night Mode Time-lapse: Use Night mode for time-lapse videos by setting your iPhone on a stable surface and selecting a long exposure time.

Privacy and Security:

App Privacy Report: Check the App Privacy Report in "Settings" > "Privacy" to see how apps are using your data.

Hide My Email: In the Mail app, you can use the "Hide My Email" feature to create random email addresses for better privacy.

Accessibility Features:

Magnifier and Magnifying Glass: Enable the Magnifier in "Settings" > "Accessibility" > "Magnifier" to use your iPhone as a magnifying glass.

Back Tap: Set up Back Tap gestures in "Settings" > "Accessibility" > "Touch" to perform actions with double or triple taps on the back of your iPhone.

AR and Augmented Reality Apps:

Measure App: Use the Measure app to measure objects and distances using augmented reality.

ARKit Apps: Explore AR apps that offer interactive and immersive experiences, such as AR games and educational tools.

iOS Updates and New Features

Apple regularly releases iOS updates, introducing new features and improvements to your iPhone's performance and functionality. Staying up-to-date with these updates ensures you're getting the best experience possible. Here's how to manage iOS updates and explore new features:

Checking for Updates:

To check for available iOS upgrades, navigate to "Settings" > "General" > "Software Update." If an update is available, tap "Download and Install."

Automatic Updates:

Enable automatic updates in "Settings" > "General" > "Software Update" > "Customize Automatic Updates" to have your device download and install updates overnight.

Exploring New Features:

Whenever a new iOS update is released, Apple provides release notes detailing the new features and improvements. Explore these notes to discover what's new.

App Privacy Report (iOS 15 and later):

In iOS 15 and later, the App Privacy Report in "Settings" > "Privacy" provides insights into how often apps have accessed your data.

Focus Mode (iOS 15 and later):

Focus mode allows you to customize notification settings based on your activity or location. You can configure it in "Settings" > "Focus."

Live Text (iOS 15 and later):

Live Text allows you to interact with text in photos and images. Simply tap on recognized text to copy, look up, or translate it.

FaceTime Enhancements (iOS 15 and later):

iOS 15 introduces FaceTime features like Share Play for synchronized content sharing and spatial audio for immersive conversations.

App Library Improvements (iOS 15 and later):

In iOS 15 and later, you can customize the organization of your apps in the App Library and add apps to the Home Screen.

Privacy Dashboard (iOS 15 and later):

The Privacy Dashboard provides a summary of how often apps have accessed sensitive data like location, photos, and microphone.

Widget Customization:

In iOS 14 and later, you can add and customize widgets on your Home Screen for quick access to app information and updates.

App Clips (iOS 14 and later):

App Clips allow you to use a small part of an app without downloading the full app. Scan App Clip codes or tap NFC tags to access them.

CarPlay Updates:

If you use CarPlay, stay updated with iOS updates to access new CarPlay features and improvements.

Keeping your iPhone's operating system up-to-date ensures you have access to the latest features, performance improvements, and security updates. Exploring new features and advanced tips and tricks can help you make the most of your device's capabilities and enhance your overall iPhone experience.

In this guide, we've delved into the advanced features and shortcuts that can streamline your interactions with your iPhone 15. We've also discussed the importance of staying up-to-date with iOS updates and exploring new features as they become available. By applying these tips and tricks, you can unlock the full potential of your iPhone and enjoy a more efficient and enjoyable user experience.

Accessories and Add-Ons

Accessories and add-ons can enhance your iPhone 15 experience, providing additional functionality, protection, and customization. In this comprehensive guide, we'll discuss recommended accessories, connecting to other devices, and utilizing third-party apps and accessories to maximize the capabilities of your iPhone.

Recommended Accessories

When it comes to enhancing your iPhone experience, the right accessories can make a significant difference. Here are some recommended accessories that can complement your iPhone 15:

Protective Cases:

A protective case is essential to safeguard your iPhone from drops, scratches, and dust. Choose a case that suits your style and provides adequate protection.

Screen Protectors:

Screen protectors help prevent scratches and protect your iPhone's display. They come in various materials, including tempered glass and plastic films.

Charging Accessories:

Invest in high-quality charging accessories, such as Apple's MagSafe charger or a wireless charging pad that supports fast charging.

A portable power bank is handy for on-the-go charging, ensuring you never run out of battery.

Headphones and Earbuds:

Enjoy immersive audio experiences with headphones or earbuds. Apple's AirPods series and other reputable brands offer various options.

External Speakers:

Portable Bluetooth speakers can enhance your audio experience when sharing music or watching videos with friends.

Car Accessories:

Car mounts and chargers make it convenient to use your iPhone while driving for navigation or hands-free calling.

Camera Accessories:

Enhance your photography skills with accessories like clip-on lenses, tripods, and gimbals for stabilized video recording.

Smartwatch:

Consider pairing your iPhone with a compatible smartwatch to access notifications, track fitness, and monitor your health.

Apple Pencil (for supported models):

If you have an iPhone that supports Apple Pencil, it's a versatile tool for note-taking, drawing, and creative tasks.

External Storage:

Expand your iPhone's storage capacity with external storage devices that connect via Lightning or USB-C.

Gaming Controllers:

Gaming controllers can enhance your gaming experience on your iPhone, especially for console-like games.

Connecting to Other Devices

Your iPhone 15 can connect to various other devices, expanding its capabilities and compatibility. Here's how to connect to some common devices:

Bluetooth Accessories:

Pair your iPhone with Bluetooth devices like headphones, speakers, keyboards, and fitness trackers. Go to "Settings" > "Bluetooth" to connect and manage these devices.

Car Connectivity:

Connect your iPhone to your car's infotainment system via Bluetooth or USB to access calls, music, and navigation while driving.

Smart Home Devices:

Set up and control smart home devices like lights, thermostats, and locks using Apple's Home app and Siri voice commands.

Apple Watch:

Pair your iPhone with an Apple Watch for fitness tracking, notifications, and quick access to apps.

AirPods and Other Wireless Earbuds:

Open the lid of your AirPods case near your iPhone to initiate the pairing process. Once paired, they will automatically connect when you use them. +

Apple TV:

Use AirPlay to mirror your iPhone's screen or stream content to your Apple TV. Verify that the WiFi networks of the two devices are the same.

Mac and iPad:

Continuity features like Handoff and Universal Clipboard allow seamless transitions between your iPhone, Mac, and iPad.

External Displays:

Connect your iPhone to external displays, projectors, or TVs using adapters or compatible cables, such as HDMI or USB-C.

Accessories with Lightning or USB-C Ports:

Many accessories, like headphones and microphones, connect to your iPhone via the Lightning or USB-C port.

Wi-Fi and Hotspot:

Use your iPhone as a mobile hotspot to share its internet connection with other devices. Activate this function by going to "Settings" > "Personal Hotspot."

Third-Party Apps and Accessories

The App Store offers a vast selection of third-party apps and accessories that can extend your iPhone's functionality:

Camera Apps:

Explore third-party camera apps that offer advanced features like manual controls, filters, and editing tools to enhance your photography.

Health and Fitness Apps:

Use third-party fitness apps to track workouts, monitor nutrition, and connect with fitness accessories like heart rate monitors and smart scales.

Smart Home Integration:

Many third-party apps and accessories work seamlessly with Apple's HomeKit framework to control and automate your smart home devices.

Audio and Music Apps:

Enhance your audio experience with third-party music streaming apps, audio editors, and equalizer apps.

Productivity Apps:

Download productivity apps that cater to your specific needs, from note-taking and task management to document editing and file management.

Gaming Accessories:

Explore gaming accessories like controllers, joysticks, and mobile gaming rigs to elevate your gaming experience.

Augmented Reality (AR) Apps:

Dive into the world of augmented reality with apps that offer immersive experiences, such as AR games, educational tools, and design apps.

External Microphones and Lenses:

Content creators can benefit from external microphones and clip-on lenses that enhance audio and photography/videography capabilities.

Accessories for Creative Professionals:

Graphic designers, artists, and videographers can find styluses, drawing tablets, and color calibration tools that complement their creative workflows.

Privacy and Security Apps:

Explore third-party apps that provide additional layers of privacy and security, including VPNs, password managers, and encryption tools.

Accessibility Tools:

Discover accessibility apps and accessories designed to assist users with specific needs, such as screen readers, communication aids, and magnifiers.

Travel and Navigation Apps:

Download travel and navigation apps that offer offline maps, translation tools, and travel guides to make your journeys smoother.

Exploring the vast ecosystem of third-party apps and accessories can help you tailor your iPhone experience to your specific interests and needs. Whether you're enhancing your productivity, expanding your creativity, or improving your health and fitness, there's likely a third-party app or accessory that can enhance your iPhone's capabilities.

In this guide, we've covered recommended accessories, how to connect your iPhone to other devices, and the wealth of third-party apps and accessories available to customize your iPhone experience. By exploring these options, you can make your iPhone 15 even more versatile and functional to suit your unique preferences and requirements.

Legal and Safety Information

Your iPhone 15 is not just a powerful tool; it also comes with legal obligations and safety considerations that you should be aware of. This guide will help you understand important legal notices and provide you with safety and regulatory information to ensure safe and responsible use of your iPhone.

Important Legal Notices

Before diving into the details, it's essential to be aware of some important legal notices associated with your iPhone 15. These notices cover various aspects of usage, intellectual property, and privacy:

Terms and Conditions:

When you set up your iPhone, you agree to Apple's Terms and Conditions. These terms outline the rules and regulations governing the use of your device, services, and software Reviewing and comprehending these words is crucial.

Privacy Policy:

Apple's Privacy Policy explains how your personal data is collected, used, and protected. It's crucial to understand how your data is handled to make informed choices about privacy settings and data sharing.

Software Licensing:

iOS and the apps on your iPhone are licensed, not sold. This means you have the right to use the software but don't own it. Unauthorized copying or distribution of apps is prohibited.

Intellectual Property:

Your iPhone and its software are protected by various intellectual property laws. You should not modify, reverse engineer, or attempt to circumvent these protections.

Export Compliance:

Your iPhone may contain encryption technology, and exporting it to certain countries may be restricted by law. Ensure compliance with your country's export regulations.

User Content:

Be aware that the content you create and share on your iPhone, such as photos, videos, and messages, may be subject to copyright and privacy laws.

Usage and Restrictions:

Apple provides guidelines on the permissible use of its products and services. Respect these guidelines to avoid legal issues.

Accessibility Laws:

Your iPhone includes accessibility features to ensure inclusivity. Familiarize yourself with accessibility laws in your region to understand your rights and responsibilities.

Safety and Regulatory Information

Your safety and the safe operation of your iPhone 15 are of paramount importance. Apple provides safety and regulatory information to help you use your device responsibly and avoid potential hazards.

Safety Guidelines:

Follow these safety guidelines when using your iPhone:

Keep your iPhone dry and away from liquids to prevent damage.

Use only Apple-approved accessories to avoid electrical hazards.

Avoid exposing your iPhone to extreme temperatures, which can affect its performance.

Don't attempt to disassemble your iPhone; it contains no user-serviceable parts.

Be cautious when using headphones or earbuds while walking or driving to maintain situational awareness.

Use caution when using your iPhone in potentially hazardous environments, such as when driving or operating heavy machinery.

Battery Safety:

Your iPhone's lithium-ion battery should be handled with care to avoid overheating, fire, or injury.

Use only Apple or Apple-certified chargers and cables.

Keep your device away from very hot or very cold temperatures.

Avoid piercing the battery or attempting to disassemble it.

If you suspect battery damage, contact Apple Support for assistance.

If you need to dispose of your iPhone or its battery, do so according to local regulations.

Health and Safety:

Your iPhone emits radiofrequency (RF) energy during normal operation. To minimize exposure, use your iPhone in good cellular network coverage areas, as it emits higher levels of RF energy in weak signal conditions.

Follow local regulations and guidelines regarding mobile phone usage, especially in sensitive areas like hospitals and aircraft.

To reduce the risk of distracted driving accidents, use your iPhone's hands-free features while driving, such as Siri and CarPlay.

Radio Frequency Exposure:

Your iPhone complies with international safety guidelines for RF exposure. To maintain compliance, ensure that you follow the manufacturer's recommendations for accessories, including carrying cases and holsters.

Regulatory Information:

Your iPhone bears regulatory symbols indicating compliance with specific safety and environmental standards. Familiarize yourself with these symbols, which can typically be found in the device's documentation.

Disposal and Recycling:

Your iPhone, its battery, and its accessories should be disposed of and recycled responsibly. Many regions have recycling programs or drop-off locations for electronic devices. Never put them in the trash with other household items.

Emergency Calls:

Your iPhone is capable of making emergency calls even without a SIM card or an active cellular plan. In the event of an emergency, you can call emergency services such as 911 or 112.

Accessibility and Safety:

Your iPhone includes accessibility features designed to enhance the experience for individuals with disabilities. Familiarize yourself with these features to ensure that your device is accessible and safe for everyone.

Legal Requirements:

Be aware that using your iPhone in certain ways, such as texting while driving or recording audio or video without consent in some regions, may be subject to legal restrictions and penalties.

By adhering to these safety and regulatory guidelines, you can ensure the responsible and safe use of your iPhone 15. Prioritizing safety and understanding your legal obligations helps you enjoy your device while minimizing risks and potential legal issues. Always stay informed about any updates or changes to these guidelines, as responsible usage evolves with technology and regulations.

Conclusion and Additional Resources

In this comprehensive guide, we have taken a deep dive into the world of iPhones, exploring their features, functionalities, and everything in between. As we wrap up this extensive journey, let's recap what we've covered, delve into further learning opportunities, and provide you with a handy glossary of terms to enhance your understanding of iPhones.

Wrapping Up

The iPhone Ecosystem

The iPhone, a groundbreaking creation by Apple Inc., has revolutionized the way we communicate, work, and entertain ourselves. We began our journey by understanding the various models and generations of iPhones, from the very first iPhone released in 2007 to the most recent innovations in 2023. Each iteration brought advancements in technology, design, and user experience, making the iPhone an iconic device worldwide.

We explored the hardware components of an iPhone, from its powerful A-series chipsets to its stunning Retina and OLED displays. The cameras, featuring technologies like Night Mode and ProRAW, have turned iPhones into versatile photography and videography tools. We also delved into the intricacies of iOS, the operating system that powers iPhones, and learned about essential features like Face ID, Siri, and the App Store.

iPhone Customization and Usage

Understanding how to make the most of your iPhone is crucial. We discussed various customization options, from arranging apps on your Home Screen to using Widgets and organizing your digital life. With the right settings, you can tailor your iPhone to your preferences, enhance your privacy with features like App Tracking Transparency, and manage your device usage with Screen Time.

Our exploration extended to accessibility features that empower users with disabilities, such as VoiceOver and Magnifier, making iPhones inclusive and user-friendly for everyone.

Connectivity and Services

iPhones are not just standalone devices; they are part of a broader ecosystem. We examined how your iPhone connects to the world, from using cellular and Wi-Fi networks to making calls via FaceTime and sending messages with iMessage. We also explored services like iCloud, which offers seamless data syncing across your

Apple devices, and the App Store, your gateway to millions of apps and games.

As part of the ecosystem, we discovered the power of features like AirDrop, Family Sharing, and Find My, which enhance collaboration, family connectivity, and security.

Staying Secure and Informed

In the digital age, security and privacy are top priorities. We learned how to protect our iPhones with passcodes, Face ID, and Touch ID, while also enabling features like Activation Lock and Two-Factor Authentication. Privacy settings and permissions put you in control of your data, allowing you to manage app access and safeguard your online identity.

We also explored Apple's commitment to environmental responsibility, including recycling programs and energy-efficient designs, making iPhones not only innovative but also environmentally conscious.

Creativity Unleashed

iPhones have evolved into creative powerhouses, with cameras that capture stunning photos and videos. We dived into photography modes like Portrait Mode, Night Mode, and ProRAW, unleashing your artistic potential. Cinematic Mode brought professional-grade videography to your fingertips, while augmented reality (AR) apps opened up new dimensions of interactive experiences.

Additionally, we explored the world of productivity with features like Siri Shortcuts, Widgets, and multitasking capabilities, turning your iPhone into a versatile tool for work and leisure.

Troubleshooting and Maintenance

Even the most advanced devices encounter issues from time to time. We discussed common iPhone problems and how to troubleshoot them, from app crashes to connectivity issues. Understanding how to perform a force restart or use Recovery Mode can be invaluable in times of need.

Regular maintenance, such as updating your iOS, managing storage, and cleaning your device, ensures that your iPhone runs smoothly and efficiently throughout its lifespan.

Further Learning and Resources

Mastering Your iPhone

While this guide provides a comprehensive overview, there is always more to discover about iPhones. Apple offers a wealth of resources to help you master your device:

Apple's Official Website: Visit Apple's website for the latest information on iPhone models, iOS updates, and user guides.

Apple Support: Explore the Apple Support website for troubleshooting guides, FAQs, and access to the Apple community.

YouTube Tutorials: YouTube is home to numerous iPhone tutorial channels, offering tips and tricks for users of all skill levels.

iOS App Store: Discover new apps and games that enhance your iPhone experience. Explore categories like Productivity, Health & Fitness, Entertainment, and more.

Apple Books: Download eBooks and audiobooks that cover a wide range of iPhone topics, from beginner's guides to advanced tips and tricks.

Online Courses and Communities

Beyond Apple's resources, you can find online courses and communities dedicated to iPhone enthusiasts:

Coursera and Udemy: These platforms offer courses on iPhone photography, iOS app development, and advanced iPhone usage.

Reddit: Join the iPhone subreddit to engage with fellow iPhone users, share experiences, and seek advice.

Stack Exchange: Visit Stack Exchange's iPhone section to ask questions, share knowledge, and troubleshoot issues.

Apple Developer: If you're interested in iOS app development, check out the Apple Developer website for resources, tutorials, and documentation.

Books and Publications

Consider exploring books and publications related to iPhones and iOS:

"iPhone User Guide for iOS": Apple regularly releases user guides tailored to specific iOS versions. These are available for free on the Apple Books Store.

"iPhone: The Missing Manual": This book by David Pogue offers comprehensive coverage of iPhones and iOS.

Tech Magazines: Magazines like "Macworld" and "iPhone Life" provide reviews, tips, and news about Apple products and services.

Glossary of Terms

To conclude our journey, here's a glossary of key terms and concepts related to iPhones:

A

Activation Lock: A security feature that prevents unauthorized use of your iPhone if it's lost or stolen.

AirDrop: A feature that allows the wireless transfer of files, photos, and more between Apple devices.

AirPods: Apple's wireless earbuds designed for use with iPhones.

AirPods Pro: Apple's premium wireless earbuds with noise-canceling features.

App Store: Apple's digital distribution platform for downloading and installing apps and games.

B

Back Tap: A feature that allows you to perform actions by tapping the back of your iPhone.

C

CarPlay: A system that integrates your iPhone with your car's infotainment system, providing access to calls, navigation, and entertainment.

Cinematic Mode: A camera mode that creates professional-looking depth-of-field effects in videos.

D

Depth Sensor: A camera feature that measures depth information for portrait and augmented reality effects.

F

Face ID: A facial recognition system used for unlocking your iPhone and authorizing purchases.

Family Sharing: A feature that allows family members to share purchased apps, media, and subscriptions.

Find My: A feature that allows you to locate your lost or stolen iPhone.

H

HDR: High Dynamic Range, a camera feature that captures more details in photos with varying light levels.

I

iCloud: Apple's cloud storage and syncing service, which allows you to store data and content across your Apple devices.

iCloud Backup: A feature that automatically backs up your iPhone's data and settings to Apple's cloud storage service.

iMessage: Apple's messaging service that allows users to send text, images, videos, and more to other Apple devices.

iOS: The operating system that powers iPhones and other Apple devices.

K

Keychain: A feature that stores and syncs passwords, payment information, and other secure data across your Apple devices.

M

MagSafe: A magnetic system that allows you to attach accessories, chargers, and cases to your iPhone.

Multitasking: The ability to run and switch between multiple apps on your iPhone.

N

Night Mode: A camera mode that enhances low-light photography.

P

Passcode: A numeric or alphanumeric code used to unlock your iPhone for added security.

Portrait Mode: A camera mode that blurs the background to emphasize the subject.

ProRAW: A file format that captures and stores photos in a format that provides more editing flexibility.

ProRes: A high-quality video format for professional video production.

R

Retina Display: Apple's branding for high-resolution displays with vivid colors.

S

Screen Time: A feature that helps you manage your device usage and set limits for certain apps and activities.

Siri: Apple's virtual assistant that responds to voice commands and provides information and assistance.

Siri Shortcuts: Custom voice commands that trigger a sequence of actions.

Wi-Fi Calling: A feature that allows you to make calls over Wi-Fi networks when cellular reception is poor.

T

Touch ID: A biometric fingerprint recognition system used for unlocking your iPhone and authorizing purchases.

True Tone Display: A feature that adjusts the color temperature of the display to match the ambient lighting.

U

Ultra-Wide Lens: A camera feature that captures a wider field of view in photos and videos.

V

Voice Control: A feature that allows you to control your iPhone using voice commands.

VoiceOver: An accessibility screen reader that reads aloud on-screen text and elements.

W

Widgets: Interactive elements and information displayed on your Home Screen.

With this glossary and the knowledge gained from this guide, you are well-equipped to navigate the world of iPhone 15 with confidence and expertise. Whether you're a seasoned iPhone user or embarking on your Apple journey, there's always more to explore, discover, and enjoy. Stay curious, stay connected, and make the most of your iPhone experience.